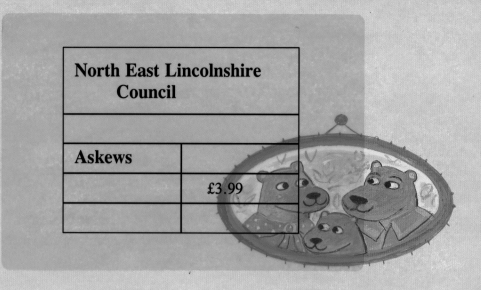

**To Doug, Alistair and Stewart - MT**
**To Alan, Maddie and Aidan - EW**
**To Eva and Iris - OR**

**About the authors:** Marie Thom and Elizabeth Walton met at a local toddler group whilst on career breaks from teaching. Before long they were running the group and had initiated a weekly craft activity which proved incredibly popular. Having searched without success for craft books suitable for this age group, they decided to write their own series!

First published in the United Kingdom in 2005 by Ragged Bears Publishing Limited, Milborne Wick, Sherborne, Dorset DT9 4PW
www.raggedbears.co.uk

Distributed by Ragged Bears Limited, Nightingale House, Queen Camel, Somerset BA22 7NN. Tel: 01935 851590

ISBN HB 1 85714 333 7

PB 1 85714 334 5

Printed in China

# Little Fingers
# Make
# Fairy
# Tales

## Ten very easy crafts for toddlers

# Little Fingers
# Make
# Fairy
# Tales

## Ten very easy crafts for toddlers

by Marie Thom
and Elizabeth Walton

Illustrated by Olivia Rayner

**RAGGED BEARS**

# Your toddler will love Little Fingers craft activities, and so will you!

## Make the world of fairy tales come to life!

**Little Fingers Make Fairy Tales** is the second in a unique series of books designed specifically for toddlers to build their very own crafts with the minimum of fuss and maximum of enjoyment.

We all know that gluing, sticking and colouring are great fun and do not necessarily need a purpose. However, the craft activities in this book channel these skills into a finished product and, very importantly, give your toddler a new and very individual relationship with much loved fairy tales.

Beautifully illustrated and with very simple instructions, all you have to do is cut out the shapes and then get your toddler creating their very own interpretation of their favourite fairy tale.

In addition, **Little Fingers** craft activities have a wealth of educational benefits for your toddler.

## Each craft :

- develops hand/eye co-ordination, spatial awareness and fine motor skills.
- encourages the following of simple directions and seeing something through to completion.
- introduces colour recognition, counting skills and working with different textures and media.
- gives your child a sense of achievement. The finished product may not look like Cinderella's shoe to you, but to your toddler that's exactly what it is!

All of the activities in these books have been road tested by a large group of toddlers ranging in age from 18 months to 4 years and their grown-ups.

# You will need:

- Coloured:
  - paper
  - card
  - crepe paper
  - gummed paper
  - tissue paper
- Cotton wool
- Doilies
- Gummed stars
- Small cardboard tube
- Silver kitchen foil
- Non-toxic glue
- Scissors (for adult to cut out shapes)
- Washable felt-tips or crayons

# A word to the adult!

There's nothing difficult about sourcing any of the materials needed in this book. You should be able to get everything from your local supermarket or stationer.

All the crafts, when done with children under the age of three, must be carried out under adult supervision. Special care should be taken when using sharp equipment, and with small objects that may cause choking. All crafts will require a small amount of adult input before the child can begin: e.g. cutting out shapes and cutting up crepe/tissue paper. You certainly don't have to be an artist to do these crafts. All the shapes are simple and straightforward to copy, draw and cut out and you don't need to be too precise in the way you do it!

**Little Fingers** crafts can be enjoyed by older children as well. We have included extension activities for the pre-school child (3-5 years old) which require some additional materials:

- Coloured feathers  • Glitter  • Lolly sticks  • Small cardboard box (e.g. cereal box)  • Wool

# Other books in the series: Little Fingers Make Nursery Rhymes

*Sarah, mother of Hannah (aged 2 years 10 months) said, 'Hannah loved doing the crafts after we'd read the nursery rhymes and fairy tales. The activities really made the stories and rhymes come to life for her!'*

*Kroo, mother of Nikhil (aged 3¹/₂) and Jay (aged 2) said, 'Art was my worst subject at school. but these crafts are so simple and self-explanatory that even I feel confident doing them with my children. We love them!'*

Think of the enjoyment you and your toddler will have together as you read and make each fairy tale! There's no mess involved – just lots of fun!

# Examples of work done by a group of toddlers.

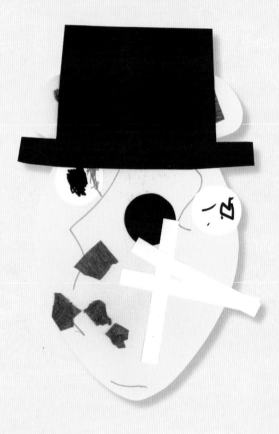

Town mouse from The Town Mouse & The Country Mouse by Aidan, aged 3.

*Aidan said, 'I liked making the funny whiskers on my mouse.'*

Jack's Beanstalk from Jack and the Beanstalk by Rebecca, aged 2 years 11 months.

*Rebecca said, 'This is brilliant! I like gluing and sticking.'*

Shoe from Cinderella
by Hannah, aged
2 years 8 months.

*Hannah said,*
*'Now I can give*
*Cin'rella her shoe!'*

Little Pig's House
from The Three
Little Pigs by
Stewart, aged
2 years 2 months.

*Stewart said,*
*'My house is funny!'*

# Get those little fingers working!

# Cinderella

Cinderella was very sad. She had to do all the jobs around the house including the cooking and cleaning.

One day there was a big dance at the Palace because the prince wanted to find a lady to marry. Everyone was going, except for Cinderella. As she sat crying in the kitchen, her fairy godmother suddenly appeared. Using magic, the fairy made Cinderella a beautiful dress and turned a pumpkin into a coach. Cinderella went to the Palace and danced all night with the prince. Of course he fell in love with her!

Unfortunately, Cinderella had to be home by midnight. As she ran back to her coach she lost one of her shoes. The prince found the shoe and searched the town to find Cinderella. When he found her, the prince was very glad, and so was she. They got married and lived happily ever after!

**Can you make Cinderella a really pretty shoe?**

Shoe

## What you need

- Background paper
  – any colour you want
- Coloured card
- Matching coloured crepe paper
  (cut into pieces)
- Black crepe paper (cut into pieces)

- Gummed stars
- Silver kitchen foil (cut into pieces)
- Glue and scissors
- A grown-up to help you do the
  cutting out. Use the shape
  opposite to guide you.

## How to do it

- Cut out the shoe from coloured card.

**Now look at the picture below. Are you ready to make
your very own shoe for Cinderella?**

- Stick the shoe on to the background paper.
- Decorate the shoe with coloured crepe paper, stars and foil.
- To finish your shoe off, cover the heel with black crepe paper.

## Suggestions for older children:

- Add glitter to the shoe.

# The Enormous Turnip

A farmer grew lots of turnips in his field. Usually all his turnips were the same size, but one day something strange happened. One of the turnips grew so big that the farmer couldn't pull it out of the ground. He needed help!

Everyone joined in to try and pull the enormous turnip up – the farmer, the farmer's wife, a boy, a girl, a dog, a cat and a mouse. They heaved and heaved and at last, together, they managed to pull it out of the ground!

The farmer was so pleased, he rushed home and made it into an enormous turnip stew and invited everyone to have a lovely plateful.

**Who is going to help pull your turnip out of the ground?**

Turnip

Leaf x2

## What you need

- Beige or cream card
- Purple and white crepe paper (cut into pieces)
- Green paper
- Glue and scissors
- A grown-up to help you do the cutting out. Use the shapes opposite to guide you.

## How to do it

- First, cut out the turnip from beige or cream card. Then cut out two strips from the green paper to make the leaves.

**Now look at the picture below. Are you ready to make your very own enormous turnip?**

- Stick purple crepe paper to the top half of the turnip.
- Stick white crepe paper to the bottom half of the turnip.
- To finish off your turnip, stick green strips on to the top and make into loops for leaves.

## Suggestions for older children:

- Use green wool to make the leaves on top of the turnip.

# Jack and the Beanstalk

Jack and his mum were very poor. So Jack was sent off to market to sell their cow. Before he got to the market, he met a man who bought the cow from Jack. He didn't give Jack money though; he gave him a handful of beans! Jack's mum was very cross and threw the beans into a field.

Overnight the beans grew into a huge beanstalk. In the morning, Jack climbed to the top of it. He found a magical land with a giant, and a hen that laid golden egg

Clever Jack managed to get the hen away from the giant and quickly climbed back down the beanstalk. Jack and his mum were never poor again!

**How tall can you make your beanstalk?**

Stalks x4      Leaf x several

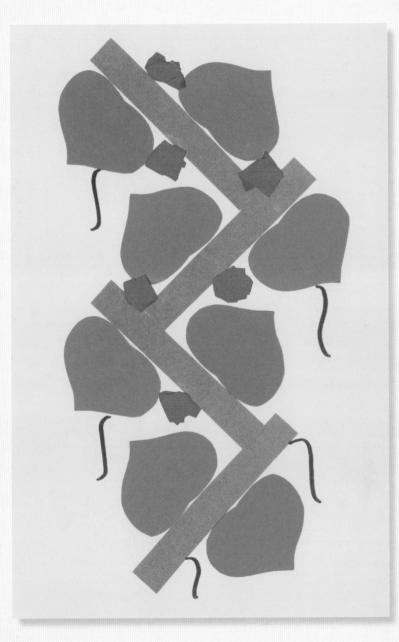

## What you need

- Blue paper for background
- Green and brown paper
- Red crepe paper
  (cut into pieces)
- Green felt-tip or crayon
- Glue and scissors
- A grown-up to help you do
  the cutting out. Use the
  shapes above to guide you.

## How to do it

- Cut out four pieces of stalk
  from brown paper and several
  leaves from green paper.

**Now look at the picture
opposite. Are you ready
to make your very
own beanstalk?**

- Stick the pieces of stalk on
  to the background paper.
- Stick the leaves to
  the beanstalk.
- Scrunch up red crepe paper
  for flowers and stick them
  next to the leaves.
- Finish off your beanstalk
  by using a green pen or
  crayon to draw the beans
  hanging down.

## Suggestions for older children:

- Use pieces of green wool to make beans.
- Use lolly sticks to make the beanstalk.

# The Little Red Hen

The Little Red Hen asked her friends to help her bake some bread. There was so much to do! She needed to plant the wheat and take care of it as it grew. When it was ready, she had to collect the grain and take it to the miller, who would grind it into flour. Only then would she be able to bake her loaf of bread.

Her friends were all too lazy to help though, so she did it all on her own. Once her friends smelt the loaf cooking they soon came round to her house wanting to help her eat it. How cheeky!

The Little Red Hen ate it up all on her own and enjoyed every mouthful!

**Your hen could be red – or any colour you want!**

Hen

Leg x2

Feet x2

Wing x2

Tail Feathers

## What you need

- Red card
- Brown and yellow paper
- Doilies
- Orange tissue paper (cut into pieces)
- Coloured paper
- Black felt-tip or crayon
- Glue and scissors
- A grown-up to help you do the cutting out. Use the shapes opposite to guide you.

## How to do it

- First, cut out the hen from red card. Now cut two legs from brown and two feet from yellow paper. Cut the wings from the doilies. Finally, cut strips of coloured paper for the tail feathers and curl round a pencil.

**Now look at the picture below. Are you ready to make your very own hen?**

- Stick the legs to the hen and the feet to the legs.
- Stick the wings on to the hen.
- Scrunch up tissue and stick to the hen's beak.
- Stick tail feathers on to the tail.
- Finish off your hen by drawing in an eye and an outline of the face.

## Suggestions for older children:

- Use lolly sticks instead of paper for legs.
- Use coloured feathers for the tail.

# The Town Mouse & The Country Mouse

There once were two mice who were cousins. One lived in the town and one lived in the countryside. They both thought that the other mouse might live in a better place, so they decided to visit each other.

The town mouse found that the countryside was too quiet. The country mouse found that the town was too noisy. So they decided to go back to their own houses where they both lived happily ever after!

**Which will you make – a town mouse or a country mouse?**

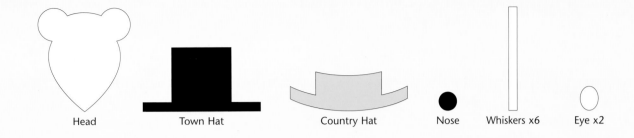

Head      Town Hat      Country Hat      Nose      Whiskers x6      Eye x2

## What you need

- White or cream card
- Black card for the town mouse's hat or yellow card for the country mouse's hat
- Black and white paper
- Brown crepe paper (cut into pieces)
- Pink crepe paper (cut into pieces)
- Black felt-tip or crayon
- Glue and scissors
- A grown-up to help you do the cutting out. Use the shapes above to guide you.

## How to do it

- First, cut out the mouse's head from white or cream card. Now, choose which mouse you are going to make and cut out the hat from either black or yellow card. Cut out the nose from black paper and the eyes from white. Finally, cut out six strips of white paper for whiskers and curl round a pencil.

**Now look at the picture opposite. Are you ready to make your very own mouse?**

- Stick brown crepe paper to your mouse's face, and add pink crepe paper to the centre of the ears.
- Stick eyes, nose and whiskers to the face.
- Draw in the centre of the eyes.
- Finish off your mouse by adding a top hat for the town mouse, or a straw hat for the country mouse.

## Suggestions for older children:

- Use wool for whiskers.

# The Elves and the Shoemaker

Once there was a shoemaker who was very poor and only had enough leather to make one more pair of shoes. He cut out the leather and went up to bed.

During the night, two elves came to his shop and made the leather into a beautiful pair of shoes. In the morning, the shoemaker was amazed! He quickly sold the shoes in his shop.

Every night after that, the elves came back to the shop to make more shoes for the shoemaker to sell. At last, the shoemaker wasn't poor any more.

To thank the elves, the shoemaker made them each a lovely set of new clothes to wear.

**What colour clothes are you going to make for your elf?**

Body  Arm x2  Leg x2  Hat  Belt  Face

## What you need

- Small cardboard tube
- Pink card
- Black and coloured paper
- Silver kitchen foil (cut into a small square for belt buckle)
- Piece of tissue paper (any colour)
- Blue, red & black felt-tips or crayons
- Glue and scissors
- A grown-up to help you do the cutting out. Use the shapes above to guide you.

## How to do it

- First, cut a wide strip from coloured paper to wrap around and cover the tube. Now cut two arms, two legs and the hat from coloured paper. Cut the belt from the black paper. Finally, cut out the face from pink card.

**Now look at the picture opposite. Are you ready to make your very own elf?**

- Wrap the coloured paper around the tube and stick it down.
- Stick the arms and legs on.
- Wrap the belt round the middle of your elf and add the silver buckle.
- Stick scrunched up tissue paper to top of the hat and stick hat to the face.
- Draw eyes, nose and a mouth on to the face.
- Finish off your elf by sticking his face on top of his body.

## Suggestions for older children:

- Add hands and feet cut out from pink card.

# Goldilocks

One day, a little girl called Goldilocks went for a walk in the woods. She found a lovely little cottage. She went in and on the table were three bowls of porridge. One was too hot, one was too salty, but the smallest one was just right. So she ate it all up!

Next, she saw three chairs. One was too high, one was too hard, but the smallest one was just right. She was too big for it though and it broke! So, she went upstairs and saw three beds. One was too hard, one was too soft, but the smallest one was just right. In she climbed and fell fast asleep.

Now, this cottage belonged to three bears. When they came home and found Goldilocks asleep they were very cross! She woke up, saw the bears and ran as fast as she could all the way home!

**Can you make a lovely big
bowl of porridge?**

Bowl

Spoon

## What you need

- Background paper
  – any colour you want
- Coloured paper
- Cotton wool
- Silver kitchen foil (cut into pieces)
- Coloured felt-tip pens or crayons
- Glue and scissors
- A grown-up to help you do the cutting out. Use the shapes opposite to guide you.

## How to do it

- First, cut out the bowl from coloured paper. When your toddler has added the porridge to the bowl, draw the outline of the spoon handle.

**Now look at the picture below. Are you ready to make your very own porridge bowl?**

- Stick the bowl on to the background paper.
- Stick cotton wool on for porridge.
- Fill spoon outline with foil.
- Finish off your bowl by decorating it using coloured felt-tips or crayons.

## Suggestions for older children:

- Use black wool to make the outline of the spoon handle.

# The Three Little Pigs

One day, three little pigs decided to leave home and build houses of their very own. One built his house with straw, one built his house with sticks and one built his house with bricks.

Suddenly the big, bad wolf came along – he wanted to catch the pigs! He blew down the house of straw and the pig ran to the house of sticks. Next, he blew down the house of sticks, so both the pigs ran to the house of bricks. The wolf tried and tried, but could not blow down the house of bricks.

He decided to climb down the chimney, but the clever pigs put a pan of hot water underneath. When the wolf came down he burnt his bottom, ran away and was never seen again.

**What is your house going to be made out of?**

House

Window x2

Door

## What you need

- Brown and black paper
- Straw house: yellow gummed paper (cut into long & short strips)
- Stick house: brown gummed paper (cut into long & short strips)
- Brick house: brown crepe paper
- (cut into pieces) and red gummed paper (cut into pieces)
- Glue and scissors
- A grown-up to help you do the cutting out. Use the shapes opposite to guide you.

## How to do it

- First, cut out the house from brown paper. Then cut two windows and a door from the black paper. Now choose which house you are going to make!

**Now look at the picture below. Are you ready to make your very own house?**

- Stick windows and door to the house.
- For the straw house, cover the roof with the short strips and the house with the long strips of yellow gummed paper.
- For the stick house, cover the roof with the short strips and the house with the long strips of brown gummed paper.
- For the brick house, cover the roof with the red gummed paper and the house with the brown crepe paper.

## Suggestions for older children:

- Make two of the same house. Stick them on to opposite sides of a small cardboard box (e.g. cereal box) to make a 3D house.

# The Ugly Duckling

A mother duck was sitting on her eggs, waiting patiently. At last, they started to hatch and lots of lovely fluffy yellow ducklings appeared. Then the last egg hatched. What a surprise – out came a duckling that was big, grey and ugly! The mother duck didn't like him one little bit. All the other ducks in the duck pond laughed and pecked at the grey duckling, until he ran away.

Wherever the duckling went, everyone he met laughed and called him ugly. He was very sad. Finally he hid in the marsh and stayed there through Winter.

When Spring came the duckling spread his wings and flew down to the pond. He saw his reflection in the water and couldn't believe it! He had turned into a beautiful white swan!

**Can you make a really beautiful white swan?**

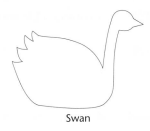

Swan

Feather x several

## What you need

- Blue paper for background
- White paper
- Orange and black tissue paper (cut into pieces)
- Black felt-tip or crayon
- Glue and scissors
- A grown-up to help you do the cutting out. Use the shapes opposite to guide you.

## How to do it

- First, cut out the swan from white paper. Now cut out broad strips of white paper and then cut slits into them to make feathers. Curl feathers round a pencil.

**Now look at the picture below. Are you ready to make your very own swan?**

- Stick the swan to the background paper.
- Cover swan's body with feathers.
- Scrunch up black tissue and stick on for an eye.
- Scrunch up orange tissue and cover the beak.
- Finish off your swan picture by drawing on a wavy line to show the top of the water.

## Suggestions for older children:

- Add reeds to the picture using green wool.
- Cover water with cut up pieces of blue crepe paper.

# The Three Billy Goats Gruff

The three Billy Goats Gruff lived in a field beside a river. Across the river they could see a bigger field full of fresh green grass that looked delicious. To get to the field they would have to cross a wooden bridge.

Under the bridge there lived an unfriendly troll. He didn't like anyone to cross over his bridge; it made him angry. The three goats decided to go over the bridge anyway. The troll tried to stop them but the biggest goat butted him right into the river.

The three Billy Goats Gruff enjoyed munching the green grass in their lovely new field.

**Is your troll going to be friendly or unfriendly?**

Face

Mouth

Nose

Teeth x3

Hair x several

Eye x2

## What you need

- Coloured card
- Green, black and white paper
- Blue gummed paper
- Coloured paper for hair
- Green tissue (cut into pieces)
- Black felt-tip pen or crayon
- Glue and scissors
- A grown-up to help you do the cutting out. Use the shapes above to guide you.

## How to do it

- First, cut the troll's face from coloured card. Now cut the mouth from black paper, the nose from green and the teeth from white. Cut strips of hair from coloured paper and curl round a pencil. Finally, cut out eyes from blue gummed paper.

**Now look at the picture opposite. Are you ready to make your very own troll?**

- Stick the mouth, nose and eyes to the troll's face.
- Add teeth to the mouth.
- Stick hair to the troll's head.
- Scrunch green tissue for warts and stick to the troll's face.
- Finish off your troll by drawing on eyebrows, nostrils, ears and the centre of the eyes.

## Suggestions for older children:

- Use wool for hair.